GREEK MYTHOLOGY

HADES,

God of the Underworld

BY JOANNA BLAIR

Enslow
PUBLISHING

Please visit our website, www.enslow.com. For a free color catalog of all our high-quality books, call toll free 1-800-398-2504 or fax 1-877-980-4454.

Cataloging-in-Publication Data
Names: Blair, Joanna.
Title: Hades, god of the underworld / Joanna Blair.
Description: Buffalo, NY : Enslow Publishing, 2027. | Series: Greek mythology | Includes glossary and index.
Identifiers: ISBN 9781978550896 (pbk.) | ISBN 9781978550902 (library bound) | ISBN 9781978550919 (ebook)
Subjects: LCSH: Hades (Greek deity)--Juvenile literature. | Gods, Greek--Juvenile literature. | Mythology, Greek--Juvenile literature.
Classification: LCC BL820.P58 B535 2027 | DDC 292.2113--dc23

Published in 2027 by
Enslow Publishing
2544 Clinton Street
Buffalo, NY 14224

Portions of this work were originally authored by Christine Ha and published as *Hades*. All new material in this edition was authored by Joanna Blair.

Cover Designer: Joshua Olson
Interior Designer: Joshua Olson
Editor: Claire Vanden Branden

Photo Credits: Cover, p. 1 Blue Diary/Shutterstock.com; pp. 4–5 delcarmat/Shutterstock.com; p. 6 Zwiebackesser/Shutterstock.com; p. 7 Ivelin Radkov/Shutterstock.com; pp. 8–9, 27 Wikimedia Commons; pp. 10–11 Zvonimir Atletic/Shutterstock.com; pp. 12–13 Vladimir Korostyshevskiy/Shutterstock.com; pp. 14–15, 29 Dima Moroz/Shutterstock.com; pp. 16–17 SergKul/Shutterstock.com; pp. 18–19 Philip Bird LRPS CPAGB/Shutterstock.com; p. 20 New Africa/Shutterstock.com; pp. 20–21 Roman Sigaev/Shutterstock.com; pp. 22–23 fritz16/Shutterstock.com; pp. 24–25 Pecold/Shutterstock.com; pp. 26–27 Andronos Haris/Shutterstock.com.

Printed in China

CPSIA compliance information: Batch #QS27ENS: For further information contact Enslow Publishing, at 1-800-398-2504.

TABLE OF CONTENTS

CHAPTER 1

RULER OF THE DEAD

Hades was the ruler of the dead. He lived in the **underworld**. The Greeks believed people's souls went there after they died.

Hades was known as the god of the underworld.

Souls crossed a river to get there. Then they faced three judges. The judges looked at each person's life. People with good lives were **rewarded**. Bad people were **punished**.

Charon carried souls across a river to the underworld on his boat.

Greek coins often had pictures of gods or famous leaders.

A FINAL FEE

Souls had to pay to cross the river to the underworld. Otherwise, they got stuck on its shores for 100 years. So, the Greeks buried people with coins in their mouths.

Legends say that Cerberus had sharp fangs.

A three-headed dog helped Hades guard the underworld. The dog's name was Cerberus. It made sure no one escaped.

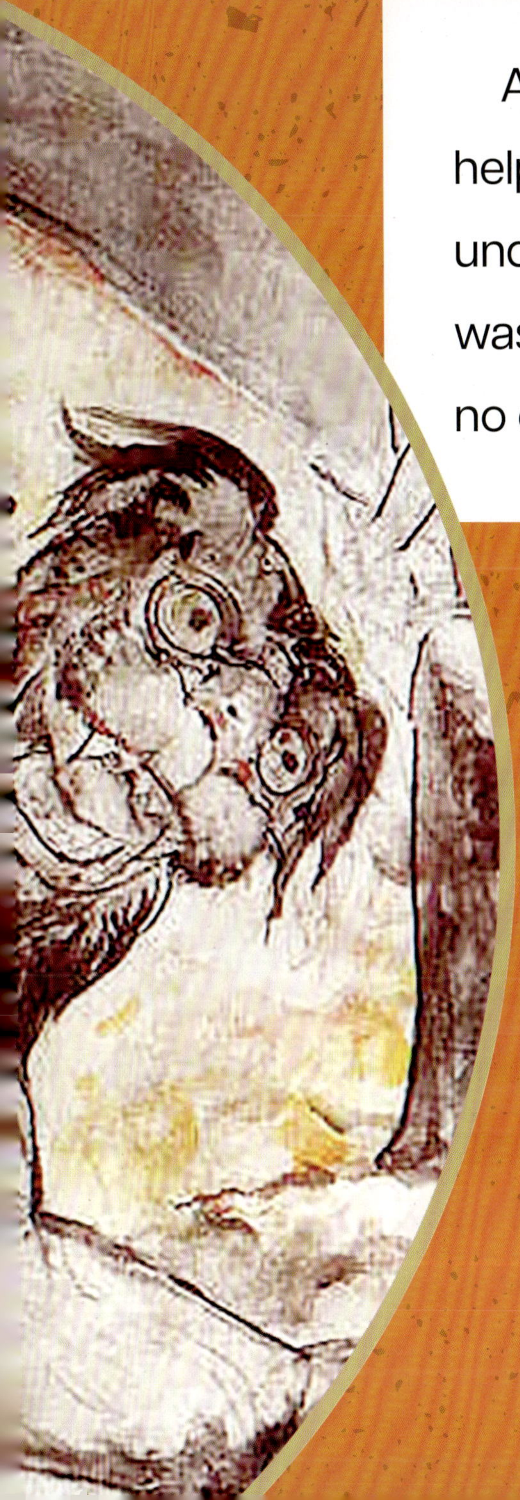

Cerberus would eat people who tried to leave the underworld.

CHAPTER 2

FAMOUS MYTHS

In one story, the Greek hero Hercules borrowed Cerberus. Hades allowed him to. But there was one rule. Hercules couldn't use weapons to take the beast.

Hercules used his super strength to capture Cerberus.

In another myth, Orpheus's wife died. He went to the underworld to get her back. Hades said she could leave. But he made a rule. The couple must leave without looking back. Orpheus looked back. So, his wife disappeared.

Orpheus was a talented musician. He sang and played the lyre.

Orpheus used music to sneak into the underworld.

The god Hermes (left) led people to the underworld after they died.

Hades, Zeus, and Poseidon once fought in a war. During it, they freed some giants. The giants gave Hades a helmet as a reward. It could make him **invisible**.

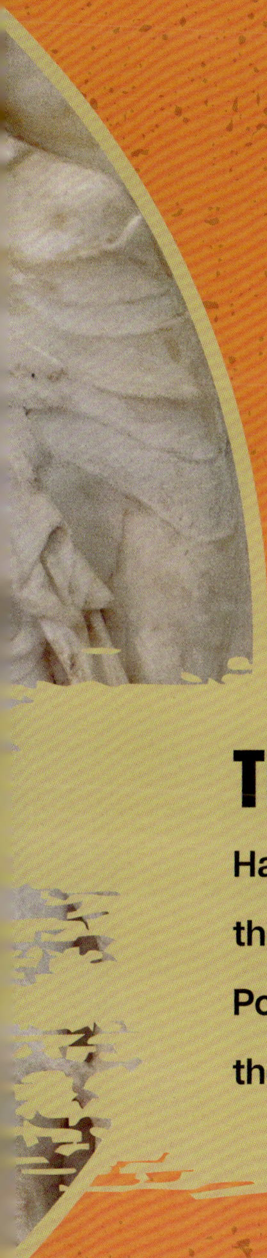

THREE KINGS

Hades and his brothers ruled the three parts of the world. Hades was king of the underworld. Poseidon controlled the oceans. Zeus ruled the skies.

CHAPTER 3

HADES'S GREAT LOVE

Hades was **stern** and serious. But in one story, he fell in love with Persephone. He brought her to his palace in the underworld.

Hades took Persephone away from her family.

Persephone's mother was heartbroken. She created a **drought**. Many people died.

Persephone was the daughter of Zeus and Demeter.

Demeter was the goddess of agriculture. She had power over plants and farming.

According to myths, anyone who ate food in the underworld had to stay there.

Hades got Persephone to eat part of a pomegranate, so she had to stay in the underworld.

Finally, Hades let Persephone return to Earth. But she could only stay for part of the year. For the other part, she would live with Hades.

Plants grew when Persephone left the underworld.

CHANGING SEASONS

The myth of Persephone explained the seasons. Winter happened when she was in the underworld. Spring came when she returned. Flowers blossomed. Plants grew.

CHAPTER 4

FEAR OF HADES

Hades had few temples. And he was not often shown in art. However, he was greatly **respected**.

The Greeks believed some temples of Hades held doors to the underworld.

In art, Hades is often shown with Persephone and Cerberus.

Many people feared Hades. Unlike other gods, he rarely responded to prayer or **sacrifices**. Like death, he usually couldn't be changed.

HADES IN ART

When he is shown in art, Hades usually holds one of two things. The first is a key to the underworld. The second is a spear. It has two sharp points.

Some Greeks refused to say his name out loud. They feared it would cause death. Instead, they used other names to **refer** to Hades. One was Plouton. This name means "wealthy."

A place dedicated to Hades was sometimes called a ploutonion.

The Romans had their own versions of the Greek gods. In Rome, Hades was known as Pluto.

The name Hades means "the unseen one."

TEST YOUR KNOWLEDGE

Take this quiz to test your knowledge.

1. Write a couple sentences describing the main ideas of Chapter 4.

2. Do you think it was fair for Hades to punish Orpheus's wife when Orpheus looked back? Why or why not?

3. Who did Hades fall in love with?

    A. Demeter
    B. Persephone
    C. Hercules

4. Why didn't Hades appear in much Greek art?

    A. The Greeks did not believe in Hades.
    B. The Greeks did not respect Hades.
    C. The Greeks were afraid of Hades.

5. What does **musician** mean in this book?

*Orpheus was a talented **musician**. He sang and played the lyre.*

A. a person who makes food
B. a person who makes music
C. a person who dislikes music

6. What does **blossomed** mean in this book?

*Spring came when she returned. Flowers **blossomed**. Plants grew.*

A. had open petals
B. shrank and died
C. became very cold

Answers can be found on page 32.

GLOSSARY

drought
A time of little or no rain.

invisible
Not able to be seen.

lyre
A stringed instrument that is similar to a small harp.

punished
Forced to do something hard or painful after doing something wrong.

refer
To talk about someone or something.

respected
Admired or seen as important.

rewarded
Given gifts or honors for doing good things.

sacrifices
Gifts to gods or goddesses to win their help or favor.

stern
Serious and firm, especially in making people follow the rules.

underworld
The land of the dead.

FOR MORE INFORMATION

BOOKS

Buckey, A. W. *Greek Mythology Gods*. San Diego, CA: BrightPoint Press, 2022.

Hudak, Heather C. *Hades*. Minneapolis, MN: Abdo Publishing, 2022.

WEBSITES

Britannica Kids: Hades

kids.britannica.com/kids/article/Hades/353223

Read more about Hades.

National Geographic: The Gods and Goddesses of Ancient Greece!

natgeokids.com/nz/discover/history/greece/greek-gods/

Learn more about Greek gods and goddesses.

Publisher's note to educators and parents: Our editors have carefully reviewed these websites to ensure that they are suitable for students. Many websites change frequently, however, and we cannot guarantee that a site's future contents will continue to meet our high standards of quality and educational value. Be advised that students should be closely supervised whenever they access the internet.

INDEX

Answer Key:
1. Answers will vary; 2. Answers will vary; 3. B; 4. C; 5. B; 6. A